SPIRIT ANIMALS

as guides, teachers and healers

a compilation of short stories and articles

Dr. Steven Farmer

Five Kings Press
An imprint of
Animal Dreaming Publishing

SPIRIT ANIMALS as Guides, Teachers and Healers

FIVE KINGS PRESS
An imprint of ANIMAL DREAMING PUBLISHING
PO Box 5203
East Lismore
NSW 2480
AUSTRALIA

✉ publish@animaldreamingpublishing.com
🌐 AnimalDreamingPublishing.com
🌐 FiveKingsPress.com
📷 @AnimalDreamingPublishing
f @animaldreamingpublishing
📷 @fivekingspress

Originally published by Earth magic, Inc. Publishing Company in electronic version as an e-book in 2016.
'Spirit Animals as Guides, Teachers and Healers' has been revised, reformatted and redesigned.

First published by Animal Dreaming Publishing in 2017
This edition published in 2020

Copyright text © Dr. Steven Farmer
🌐 EarthMagic.com

ISBN: 978-0-9953642-8-8

Designed by Animal Dreaming Publishing

This book is dedicated to the animals and to all the humans that love them and appreciate their innumerable gifts to us.

CONTENTS

Introduction   7

Chapter 1
Animals as Spirit Guides   11

Chapter 2
Our Kinship with Animals   17

Chapter 3
Our Natural Connection to Animals and How they
can serve as Spirit Guides   21

Chapter 4
Messages from Animal Spirit Guides   25

Chapter 5
How we get Messages from Spirit Guides   27

Chapter 6
Understanding the Messages from Animal Spirit Guides   31

Chapter 7
Power Animals   33

Chapter 8
The Hawk and the Snake   37

Chapter 9
Imagination   41

Chapter 10
The Grasshopper Sings: "Let The Song Find You"   45

Chapter 11
Why did the Tortoise cross the Road?   49

Chapter 12
Animal Spirit Guides and Ancestors   53

CONTENTS

Chapter 13
Cooper's Hawk   57

Chapter 14
The Artist and the Snake   63

Chapter 15
Animal Spirit Guides and Scuba Diving   69

Chapter 16
Hawk Pays a Visit   75

Chapter 17
'Aumakua, Familiars, and Spirit Animals ... Oh My!!!   81

Chapter 18
What did the Animals know?: Instinct, Survival,
and the Tsunami   85

Chapter 19
Pismo the Snake saves the Day   91

Chapter 20
Conversation with Turtle   95

Chapter 21
Animals, Spirit Animals, and Omens   101

Chapter 22
Raven Speaks   105

References   110

Also by the Author   111

About the Author   112

INTRODUCTION

S pirit Animals as Guides, Teachers, and Healers is a compilation of articles I've written over the last few years about a topic that is near and dear to my heart: how animals can serve as spiritual messengers to help guide, teach, and heal us. Although this subject is covered in detail in some of my books and other products, in particular the best-selling *Animal Spirit Guides* and *Pocket Guide to Spirit Animals,* editorial constraints prevented much of this material from being included in those publications. Several others have also been written since those books became available. I wanted to make the material in this book readily available and in a form that was affordable and easy to access.

There are many true to life stories of experiences with spirit animals in these pieces, and as you read through, I'm sure you'll find yourself intrigued by the entire topic. I've had many demonstrations of how the natural world communicates with us, particularly through the animals that show up in physical reality or in consciousness. To learn from these spirit beings, it's a matter of becoming better listeners with your ears, eyes, and senses.

The more you pay attention and "listen" with all of you, the more you can discern and understand their messages.

How to use this book

The first chapter is adapted from my book *Animal Spirit Guides.* I chose it to be the introduction to this series of articles as it gives a good overview of the whole subject. If this is new to you, this book is a good place to start. Even if you're familiar with the idea of spirit animals as guides, I'm sure you'll deepen your understanding of the miraculous way in which these spirit beings help us along our paths. You may choose to read straight through or pick and choose the articles that grab your interest.

These articles were written at different times and for different purposes, so there is some repetition here and there, particularly for the most important ideas, yet there is also a wealth of fresh perspectives on the magic inherent in working with animal spirit guides. For our long-ago ancestors, receiving guidance from the natural world was a given, and in some cases a necessity. Tuning into the gifts of spirit animals is arguably one of the easiest ways to open this deep ancestral memory of how to communicate with nature.

Savor the stories. Get to personally know the spirit animals described in them. Just close your eyes and use your imagination. If there's one you particularly identify with, call on that etheric form of being when you need help of any kind. Experiment with this way of viewing reality and see what happens. This is one way you can experience direct revelation: receiving messages firsthand from Spirit without an intermediary. As you'll see, animals are not only potential messengers from God, but the entire world can be—especially the natural world.

Most of all have fun and enjoy the process!

CHAPTER 1

ANIMALS AS SPIRIT GUIDES

Those spirits that are in animal form that teach us, guide us, empower us, and help us heal are called animal spirit guides or spirit animals. In shamanic and indigenous cultures they're usually called totem animals or power animals. Often these terms are used interchangeably, although there are subtle differences in meaning.

The term *totem animal* has two meanings. First, a totem animal is typically one that is shared by a family, clan, or group. In indigenous cultures, the family you were born into all has in common a totem animal. In modern societies, various groups also have communal totems, such as sports teams or clubs that identify with a totem animal. A second meaning of totem animal is a representational object of a particular animal, like the sculpted tortoise, owl, raccoon, and hawk figures sitting immediately in front of my computer. We often give our children totem animals, such as stuffed teddy bears or bunny rabbits to give them comfort.

The term *power animal* has its origins in shamanism. This is a specialized animal spirit guide the shaman or shamanic practitioner acquires early in their initiation into their practice. Their power animal travels with them whenever they go on a shamanic journey, which is an altered state of awareness in which the practitioner sends his soul or consciousness into non-ordinary reality to receive teachings, guidance, and healings. As you'll see though, a power animal is not the exclusive domain of a shaman.

Discovering your power animal

You can have a relationship with a power animal even if you're not a shaman or shamanic practitioner. We're born with one but in Western culture typically there is no support for children having that kind of relationship. The power animal that you were born with may eventually leave due to not having conscious interaction with the person to whom they're assigned. If they do leave it's usually around seven or eight years of age when a child's perspective of the world changes dramatically.

The good news is that if your power animal leaves—through no fault of your own—it may return when you're older, or a different one may come to you who's more aligned with your needs at a particular stage of your development. You may find an animal that repeatedly shows up physically and symbolically, as if beckoning you to let it become your spiritual ally. It may show up in meditations, visions, dreams, or a shamanic journey. A shamanic practitioner can do a journey on your behalf or guide you on a journey to find your primary animal spirit guide. Another option is in my book *Power Animals*, there's a CD with a guided journey to retrieve this spiritual ally. It's a highly personal and specialized relationship, one where the personality and characteristics of the particular power animal that you have attracted to you are often reflective of your own personality and characteristics.

As I mentioned, power animals can change over time depending on where you're at with your personal and spiritual development. You may have more than one at any time, each one serving a different purpose. I have four power animals with whom I have a relationship, and that's more than enough. For many years Owl spirit was my primary guide, or power animal. His "medicine" of seeing into the shadows was perfect during my years as a psychotherapist, as that process often deals with those aspects of us that are hidden from consciousness. A few years ago I closed my private practice to focus on my writing, teaching, and shamanic healing work, and since then Owl has taken a back seat, and Raven showed up as one of my main spirit guides. His medicine—magic, creativity, healing—is much more appropriate for my current mission.

Power animals as spiritual allies

Although every creature on the planet can be an animal spirit guide, domesticated animals cannot be power animals because they've lost much of their wildness and are removed from the natural world. Likewise, some traditions believe that insects are to be excluded from being power animals because of their size and nature, however I'll leave it up to the reader to discern whether that's the case. Mythological animals such as unicorns or dragons can be power animals even though they have no physical expression but exist in the collective human consciousness in an etheric form.

To experience the tremendous value of working with animal spirit guides you don't need to be a shaman, have any interest in shamanism, nor be associated with an indigenous culture. For most purposes you don't even need to be concerned as to whether you consider an animal spirit guide a totem or power animal. Instead, consider these wonderful beings as spiritual allies that want to reach out to each and everyone one of us who are open to their guidance and, when called with sincere intent, will respond.

One of the great advantages of working with animal spirit guides is that the actual animal is physically and symbolically present in so many ways throughout every society and culture on earth. Because of their abundant representations in third-dimensional reality, they're continually in our consciousness. Depending on how and in what way they show up in the material world, whether in the flesh or as a symbol, their appearance can be as a representative of the spirit of that animal.

When an animal shows up in an uncommon way or repetitively, the spirit of that animal has come to give you a message. It isn't just the single animal, or the spirit of that specific animal, but is a representative of the entire species. It's the Collective Consciousness or Oversoul of that particular species. The hummingbird that flits about and then hovers for several seconds directly in front of you isn't just a hummingbird but is carrying with her the essence of *all* hummingbirds, and is therefore Hummingbird with a capital "H." That's also why when we speak of an animal spirit guide, we leave out the "a" or "an" as a way of recognizing and honoring that spirit animal. A hawk that visited me with the message to stay focused wasn't only a hawk, but was an expression of the Collective Consciousness of all hawks, and was therefore Hawk.

Not only do these spirit animals help us in many ways, but another positive effect is that you'll deepen your appreciation for the magic and mystery of all animals' physical form, whether they are of the air, water, or the land. Every being on this beautiful and majestic planet has its place in the web of life, and as we develop our consciousness and awareness of the unique quality of animal spirit guides, we enhance our relationships with all of our animal brothers and sisters.[1]

1 Farmer, Steven, *Animal Spirit Guides,* Hay House Inc, US, 2006.

CHAPTER 2

OUR KINSHIP WITH ANIMALS

M alidoma Patrice Somé is a healer, teacher, and elder of the Dagara tribe in the small West African nation of Burkina Faso. He travels extensively giving classes and workshops, and in one of his teachings, he describes how the Dagara believe there are three levels of intelligence on Earth. Plants are considered to be the most intelligent beings, animals second, while humans capture the ribbon for third place. It's a different way of looking at life and our relationship with plants and animals, and one that contradicts the more typical and subtle arrogance ingrained within many of us in the more "civilized" societies.

Whether we agree that we're somehow less intelligent than plants or animals, most indigenous peoples, who are more intimately connected to the natural world, know that we are intrinsically related to all life on this fair planet. Chief Seattle, of the Suquamish and Duwamish tribes of British Columbia said it best:

Humankind has not woven the web of life. We are but one thread within it. Whatever we do to the web, we do to ourselves. All things are bound together. All things connect.

So how is it that those of us who have been raised in the more "civilized" parts of the world have forgotten this connection? How did we forget how to talk with the animals, to listen to their language, to connect with their spirit, and to show them compassion and gratitude for all they give us? How did we come to live in this illusion that we're somehow separate from all other beings and nature herself?

Of course there's no single cause for this dissociation from the natural world, and specifically from animals, yet we can point to a couple of powerful influences. One of these was the beginning of the scientific revolution, heralded by Sir Francis Bacon in the early sixteenth century. Considered the founder of modern science, Bacon claimed that goal seeking was a specifically human activity, and attributing goals to nature misrepresents it as human-like. It became science's job to objectify nature, and to think otherwise became a cardinal sin. Then in 1637, along came Descartes, famous for his quote: "I think, therefore I am", although perhaps it's more accurate to say: "I am, therefore I think"! Descartes maintained that only humans have souls, so animals can't really feel pain, and thus pioneered the practice of vivisection further objectifying the animal world.

In the twentieth century, many others would openly disagree with this way of thinking. Darwin was one who challenged this view and demonstrated that animals had their own unique intelligence. Yet paradoxically, in the past century and even up to today, animals have continued to be treated like objects, as having no soul or spirit, and here mainly to serve humankind's needs and purposes. Yet, thankfully, these attitudes are slowly changing.

With the spark of ancient memory awakening in many of us comes a deep longing to experience the intimacy with the natural world that was a way of life for our ancestors, who expressed their gratitude for the gifts of the earth through continuous prayer, ceremony, and ritual. They appreciated that whatever you took from nature, you always gave something back, and you used every part of what you'd taken. They knew that every aspect of life was infused with Spirit and consistently honored that fact. Animals were seen as kin, as brothers and sisters, and even when hunted for sustenance, they were honored and treated with the utmost respect and gratitude for sacrificing their lives.

Another aspect was the relationship to the spirit of these various animals. Typically a clan, tribe, or community would have a spirit animal in common, called a totem animal, one that everyone in the clan could call on for protection and guidance. Shamans in these communities typically had one or more spirit animals that they used in their work on behalf of the people called power animals. An animal spirit guide was any animal that showed itself in an unusual way or repeatedly. The animal was believed to be bringing a message from the spirit of that animal.

The purpose of my books and oracle cards is not only to help people discover how our animal brothers and sisters and their spirits can help us in our lives with guidance and healing, but also to encourage the re-awakening of that inherent connection we have to animals. As they did for our ancestors, the spirit of an animal will attempt to reach us through unusual or repetitive visitations, whether the physical animal or a symbolic representation. If a crow lands three feet away and looks at you, or a crow shows up repeatedly throughout the day, Crow spirit is trying to pass along a message. Crow may also show up symbolically such as in dreams, on a TV show, or a ceramic figure in a bookshop. Regardless of how he shows up, he may be bringing you an important message from Spirit.

I always suggest to pause and ask Crow (or whatever animal it is) what the message is before referring to any books or cards that contain possible meanings of any such sighting. Once you ask the animal, pay attention to any impressions that come to you, whether visual, auditory, thoughts, or sensations in your body. If the message isn't clear right away, often through the coming days you'll pick up other signs, omens, and insights that clarify the message from the animal spirit.

Our animal brothers and sisters want to reach us, teach us, and heal us. It's simply a matter of being open and receptive to Spirit's communication through the specific animal spirit, and doing whatever we can to maintain the awareness of our relationship with our animal brothers and sisters.

CHAPTER 3

OUR NATURAL CONNECTION TO ANIMALS
and how they can serve as spirit guides

It's amazing how animals permeate our consciousness and are with us all the time. They can show up in their physical form, like the hummingbird that flits about and blesses the flowers blooming in the yard, or the dolphins that frolic in the ocean just outside the surf. Or they can appear in symbolic form, like the tiny raccoon, tortoise, owl, and hawk totems that are sitting on my computer observing me right now, the painting of the Rainbow Serpent on my wall, or the bronze rendition of a raven with his wings spread that looks at me from the corner of the room.

This intimate connection we have to the animal kingdom shows itself in a variety of ways. Even in congested urban settings, the birds in the trees sing away, the pigeons gather around the man on the park bench feeding them, and the squirrels scamper about doing squirrel business. Taking a walk in the forest we might see rabbits darting through the bush, a quick glimpse of a deer before it charges away, or wild turkeys scratching for grubs. Dogs, cats, goldfish, and hamsters are some of the more common domesticated animals that compel us to remember this connection. Then there are zoos and wild animal parks that give us a safe and contained glimpse of the wildness that abounds in nature.

Go into any number of stores and you'll see animal icons in pictures, jewelry, and fabric. Many sports teams are named after animals, such as the Philadelphia Eagles or Sydney Roosters, as well as various organizations such as the Lion's Club or the Loyal Order of Moose. Fairy tales are filled with animals, ones that communicate readily with each other and with humans. In our everyday language, animal metaphors abound. The stock market is either a bull or a bear market, someone is as busy as a beaver, or they try to weasel their way out of things. You may be trying to outfox someone, but because your idea sounds fishy, they probably think you're just horsing around and trying to get their goat, so once they find you out, you'll have to eat crow.

Okay, enough examples. You get the picture. We're so intertwined with our animal brothers and sisters that most of the time we remain unaware of their presence in our lives and their bountiful gifts they give us.

Not only are animals around us in all these ways and more, but it's also important to recognize that we are an animal too—the human animal. We only need to pause for a few moments and feel our heart beating, notice our breathing, our movements; we also eat, sleep, eliminate, and procreate in the same basic manner as nearly all other animal beings. We breathe the same air and live together on the same planet, whether on land, in the air, or in the waters. Like every other being, we eventually die, the substance of our bodies returning to the earth as our spirit goes to the spirit world.

CHAPTER 4

MESSAGES FROM ANIMAL SPIRIT GUIDES

When an animal or a symbol of that animal shows up to you in an unusual way or repeatedly (at least three times in a short period of time) they're most definitely trying to convey a message from the spirit world to you. One year, around the winter holidays, I had a hawk that did both. He showed up three times in a short period, and in one of those visits performed the very unusual act of flying into my office. Since this was the third time he appeared, and on this time showed up in a very unusual way, it got my attention. It was evident that this was a strong message meant for me, particularly since Hawk has been a consistent and recurring animal spirit guide. I was on an important writing project and doing everything but writing. His message was clear: focus!

In another instance a friend, Melody, described how after her father's death she went to a spot on the beach located in front of her father's favorite restaurant, and a single dolphin was frolicking in the water unusually close to shore. As she walked on the beach, the dolphin followed her for several meters, then swam further out to sea and joined his pod. This was a very reassuring message from Dolphin spirit to Melody, that her father was just fine in the spirit world.

Tim and his wife Beth provide another illustration. Less than a year ago they were preparing a major move to a new city, and Tim was feeling extremely anxious about the move to the point of losing sleep and dropping weight. One night a raccoon showed up in the backyard. He looked up the message from Raccoon in my book, *Power Animals,* and discovered that the message was about resourcefulness. At that point he realized that he did in fact have all the necessary resources, both internal and external, for this move. It relaxed him a great deal and he and his wife are now living very successfully in their new home in a new city.

I've had the good fortune to have a number of personal experiences like these. I have also heard a number of stories from others of these miraculous interventions on the part of an animal spirit guide, either represented or embodied by the physical animal, or as a symbol of that animal. An example of a repetitive symbolic representation would be one where you have a vivid and colorful dream about a bear, go to the market the next day and hear two strangers in conversation talking about bears, and that evening turn on the television and there just happens to be a program about grizzly bears. An experience like this counts just as much as three literal sightings, and since most of us who live in urban areas will never actually encounter live bears or come close to a number of wild animals, the spirit of that animal has to reach us some other way to get a message across.

CHAPTER 5

HOW WE GET MESSAGES FROM SPIRIT GUIDES

There are four major ways that we get messages from the spirit world: visual, auditory, kinesthetic, or cognitive. As your receptivity to the spiritual dimension opens and develops, you'll discover that one of these pathways is the strongest and feels the most natural, with a secondary one that works fairly well. The more you practice and the more you attune to the spiritual dimension, you'll find you can receive input through the other channels as well. What's required is that you hold a clear intention to receive these messages and simply remain receptive, and they will come to you, often in unexpected and surprising ways.

The four ways are:

Visual

When you see that dolphin a few yards from shore, or the crow that lands a couple of feet away, and you know these are unusual visitations and meant for you, this is the animal spirit coming through a visual channel. *Clairvoyance* is another way; you see spirit animals that are in the non-physical realm in your mind's eye or as an apparition, such as having a vision of a bear or a mythological animal like a dragon, or having a vivid dream where a wolf makes an appearance.

Auditory

You hear the voice of an animal spirit guide in your mind giving you some advice, or when a sound in the environment triggers a thought about an animal spirit guide. Another means is for you to overhear a conversation or listen to someone talking and intuitively know that what is being said is a message from a spirit animal. Hearing spirit's communication is called *clairaudience.* Messages coming in this way are typically short and to the point, without excess verbiage.

Kinesthetic

This is when you feel or sense something, sometimes called a gut feeling and often termed intuition. You feel or sense the presence of the ethereal form of one of your more common animal spirit guides or your power animal, and get a sense of what they're trying to communicate to you. This is also called *clairsentience.*

Cognitive

This is a knowing through our thought processes, also called inspiration or insight. If your primary mode of input is through this pathway, your animal spirit guide is communicating with you by generating a thought or thought pattern, also called *claircognizance.* Often someone doesn't exactly know how they know, and, if asked, will tell you they just somehow know.

So unless you're already aware of which of these channels is your primary avenue for spiritual input, for the next several days simply observe how you make the simplest of choices. What are the most important considerations about where you live? How do you shop for things? How do you decide what to wear? As you observe yourself, you'll gradually notice the primary way or ways you connect with the spirit world.

Do you *look* for and *see* the communications from your animal spirit guide or other spirit helpers? Do you *hear* their voice? Or feel them? Or for you is it more of a contemplative and insightful process? Keep in mind which channels are your primary spiritual conduits and with practice, you'll develop greater trust in how you get messages from spirit animals.

CHAPTER 6

UNDERSTANDING THE MESSAGES FROM ANIMAL SPIRIT GUIDES

A s I've noted, when an animal shows up in ordinary reality in an uncommon way or at unusual times, such as a dove landing on the balcony two feet away, a raccoon that's walked into your back door, or a fox that darts across your path as you're walking in the woods, it's definitely a sign from that animal spirit guide. The dove may be reminding you to stay calm, the raccoon letting you know you've got what it takes, or the fox suggesting that you be discerning about who to trust. If you spot a crow in the tree outside your window three mornings in a row when there's usually no crow there, it could mean that you're going to be seeing more magic in your life. If you see a hummingbird repeatedly, she may be telling you that you need more joy and sweetness in your life.

Animal spirit guides will teach you in both cryptic and dreamlike ways and also offer their counsel by hitting you right between the eyes with a message that's obvious. However, when it isn't clear what the message is or you want to understand more about it, there are several options. One is to look for the animal in *Animal Spirit Guides, Pocket Guide to Spirit Animals,* or any other such book, or do a search on the internet and see what the possible meanings are to the visitation.

One of the most useful and direct ways is to communicate with the spirit of that animal that you've sighted and ask them what they are attempting to communicate to you. The first thing to do (unless you're driving) is to close your eyes, then imagine that animal's spirit in front of you, and in your mind ask the question: "What do you want me to know?" Take a deep breath, relax your body, and see what sort of impressions and information you get, whether visual, auditory, kinesthetic, or cognitive. Often you'll get a "hit" on what the meaning of the visitation is. By contemplating the sighting over the next few hours and letting it work, you will also be able to reveal insights about the experience. If you know how to do a shamanic journey, that's another means of understanding what the message was. The more you practice deciphering the messages, the easier it becomes.

I encourage you to practice any of these methods in addition to looking to other resources for the meaning of the spirit animal's communication to you. These remarkable beings want to help us and teach us and will do so in a myriad of ways.

CHAPTER 7

POWER ANIMALS

The term *power animal* has its origins in shamanism. This is a specialized animal spirit guide the shaman or shamanic practitioner acquires early in initiation into their practice. In addition to being available any time night or day, the shaman's power animal travels with them whenever they go on a shamanic journey. The shamanic journey is a process in which the practitioner goes into an altered state of consciousness and he sends his soul or consciousness into non-ordinary reality to receive teachings, guidance, and healings from his spirit helpers who exist in this realm.

Although, in times past, a power animal was the domain of the shaman, it's become apparent that anyone who is drawn to work with animal spirit guides can have a relationship with a power animal. You don't need to be a shaman or a shamanic practitioner, or even have a strong interest in shamanism. Everyone is born with a power animal, however our western cultural values haven't supported this idea. We're not taught about spirit animals or power animals and therefore don't pay them any attention, so after a while your power animal gets bored and leaves! Through no fault of your own, I might add.

The good news is that we can recover our power animal, or even discover a new one, by opening our hearts, minds, and souls to this notion. Your power animal may come to you in meditations, visions, dreams, or shamanic journeys. If you've had a particular affinity or attraction for an animal, it's most likely this is your power animal. Just recently someone wrote and asked what I thought her power animal was. She went on to describe how hawks have shown up for her much of her life, especially in the past few weeks, and was wondering if this could perhaps be her power animal. I wrote back and basically confirmed what she already knew, that Hawk was her main animal spirit guide, or power animal.

The power animal relationship is a highly personal and specialized relationship with an animal spirit guide. It's not one you choose in the usual sense of the word. It's more of a soul-to-soul connection, your soul bonding with the soul—or more accurately the Oversoul—of the animal. The relationship is one to be nurtured and attended to on a regular basis, and if done, will last a number of years.

Your power animal may still leave you at some point, even if you've paid attention to her over the years. That usually means the relationship has served its purpose, and another power animal either is or will be coming into your life. I've observed how these spirit guides will enter into our lives at a time when we most need their particular expression of spiritual power. For instance, if you're moving into a position of leadership, Cougar spirit may very well leap into your life as power animal, helping you with confidence and clarity in your leadership roles. If you're going through a major transformative process with big changes, you may find Snake spirit or Butterfly coming into your life as a power animal.

Another interesting facet is that often your power animal is reflective of your personality characteristics. For instance, Rachel is slight of build, energetic, with a tendency to move very quickly, often juggling several tasks at once, flitting from one to the other. It's no accident that her power animal turned out to be Hummingbird. Gary is a fairly large man, gentle by nature, yet very capable of standing up for himself or for others as needed. No one messes with him. No surprise that his power animal is Bear.

As for myself, I recently acquired Raven as a power animal—or perhaps I should say he recently acquired me! Well actually, we acquired one another through our soul connection. I am at a point in my life where he is perfect for me. Over the years I've developed relationships with three other power animals, each one for different purposes. I don't typically reveal who they are publicly as these are such highly personal and intimate relationships, and generally suggest that others do the same. Raven is the exception. In a conversation he gave me permission to talk about him as my power animal since I teach and write about these things. As for some of his characteristics, Raven tends to value his solitude, is a shapeshifter, and is a powerful manifester. He has a number of different calls or songs to communicate a variety of things, and if necessary he can be loud. Raven reflects a lot of my characteristics—or should I say, I reflect a lot of his!

Other questions that come up are about cats or dogs being

power animals. Generally domesticated animals can't be power animals because they've lost much of their wildness and are removed from the natural world. Likewise, some traditions believe that insects are to be excluded from being power animals because of their size and nature. Generally true, however in my book *Power Animals*, Dragonfly and Butterfly both argued vehemently about being included, so I caved and included them. I see now the wisdom of that, as they both offer unique types of power.

Yet another question that comes up on occasion is about mythological or etheric animals, such as dragons or unicorns. Although some would insist that they exist in third-dimensional reality, it really doesn't matter whether they do or not. If you believe they do, then they do. Any of these so-called mythological animals can certainly be your power animal. The only disadvantage is that they're not commonly seen in the physical world as are other kinds of animals.

CHAPTER 8

THE HAWK AND THE SNAKE

’ve had many experiences where Spirit has come through with messages in this way and have heard many stories from others of similar occurrences. Just recently while preparing to attend a men's group I walked out to the backyard and heard a flutter of wings coming from the trees in the neighbor's yard. At first I thought nothing of it, as it's not unusual to see crows flying about here and there. Then in a flash a different type of bird appeared, and much to my surprise and delight, it turned out to be a hawk! It was the first time ever that one showed up in our yard, so it certainly qualified as unusual. The hawk flew to the Arbutus tree directly behind the house and landed on the branch for a few moments, during which—I swear—he looked directly at me.

He didn't stay long, but long enough for me to know he was delivering a message. I closed my eyes, took a deep breath, and asked, "Hawk brother, what's your message?" Once you ask the question of the spirit animal, in this case Hawk spirit, it's important to pay attention to everything that happens following, including what you see, hear, or feel. In this case I immediately heard my inner voice, "Stay focused and pay attention for other signs," which turned out to be completely relevant for the upcoming men's group. My friend and I had offered to facilitate this particular session and since the group had been meeting for some time now, we both agreed that it was time to push the edges a bit further. We were confident the processes open the way for greater honesty and depth.

I was driving to the group thinking about what Hawk had said when I pulled up to a stoplight and looked to my left. On the side panel of the U-Haul truck two feet from me was an image of several snakes with reference to a website to "learn more about garter snakes and other animals." I was immediately reminded of the second part of Hawk's message—being alert to other signs—and once again asked for the message, this time from Snake spirit. "There's to be significant healing in the group." Okay, got it. That boosted my confidence that all will go well in the men's group today, and it helped me to relax and just show up and stay present and focused.

Without going into detail, the processes we introduced served the purpose. I was very thankful for Hawk and Snake spirit sending their representatives to me. Hawk spirit in the form of a physical hawk and Snake spirit via the symbols on the side panel of the truck, with several images of snakes as if to add to the power of that message.

If you should have a similar experience of encountering an animal in physical or symbolic form as I did, there are a few things you can do to understand and interpret the message. Here are some suggestions that I'm sure you'll find helpful.

1) Close your eyes, take a couple of nice, comfortable deep breaths, and in your mind state, "Please tell me or show me the message," then pay attention to any immediate thoughts, images, or dialogue. Trust what you get, whether or not it makes immediate sense. It will later.

2) Think of the characteristics of the actual animal. That will give a clue to the spirit animal's "medicine." For instance, a hawk has incredible eyesight and when scanning to horizon with his broader vision, when something gets his attention, he focuses. So one of Hawk spirit's medicines is the gift of focus and presence.

3) Refer to any books or other devices that give you some ideas as to the possible message, such as *Animal Spirit Guides* or the new condensed and revised *Pocket Guide to Spirit Animals.*

4) Search the internet for terms such as spirit animals, power animals, totem animals, etc. to discover what others have noted as to the message of the particular spirit animal of your inquiry.

No matter the possible interpretation or meaning of the message, be sure that it somehow resonates with your inner knowing and your heart. The more you listen, the more you will hear.

Most of all, have fun with this and be sure to thank the animals and the spirit animals in whatever way you choose.

CHAPTER 9

IMAGINATION

How many times have you heard, "Oh, it's just your imagination!" implying that it's merely some delusional artifice that holds no bearing on reality, reserved for the likes of children, artists, or writers of fiction? This phrase is useful in some instances, but limited. There's even a song by The Temptations called, "Just My Imagination," where a guy sings about his dream girl, the punch line being that he realizes he can never really have her because it's all in his imagination.

Yet our imagination is a much more powerful force than we typically give credit. For instance, when Joan of Arc was facing her inquisitors, she was asked if she believed she could hear the voice of God, to which she replied without hesitation that she did. Her inquisitor then asked her, "How do you know it's not just your imagination?" Her reply: "How else would I hear?"

Imagination is what bridges the gap between the world of spirit and the concrete reality that we see, hear, and feel within and all around us. It's with our imagination that we can contact our spirit helpers, including our animal spirit guides, in whatever form they may take. These animal spirit guides, who love us and want to help us, can show us much about our lives and our world. With an open heart and open mind, you'll find that you can receive clear messages and guidance from these wonderful spirit beings.

As I wrote in *Animal Spirit Guides*:

One of the great advantages of working with animal spirit guides is that the actual animal is physically and symbolically present in so many ways throughout every society and culture on earth. Because of their abundant representations in third-dimensional reality, they're continually in our consciousness. Depending on how and in what way they show up in the material world, whether in the flesh or as a symbol, their appearance can be as a representative of the spirit of that animal.[2]

The message is actually coming *from* the spiritual counterpart *through* the physical presence of the animal. When an animal appears repetitively or in an unusual way, he/she becomes a courier or messenger, passing along the guidance that the spirit of that animal is trying to communicate.

A friend of mine who lives in Arizona reported that a road runner walked up to her the other day, looked at her, then calmly walked away. She was imaginative enough to know that Road Runner was trying to impart some message, particularly as this bird behaved in such an unusual way. I typically suggest that if you have such an experience to

2 Farmer, Steven, *Animal Spirit Guides*, Hay House Inc, US, 2006.

take a couple of breaths, close your eyes, and "imagine" that animal in front of you. Then ask the animal, who is simply a representative of the essence of that entire species, what the message or teaching is.

Since my friend asked me in a letter, I did that on her behalf, and wrote to her this response: "Road Runner is telling you that your thoughts are racing; that you're required to be able to shift from thoughts about this or that project. Since he approached you and wasn't running, he's also saying to slow down, take the time to meditate, not by sitting but by doing a walking meditation. You feel yourself running around a lot, often at top speed, and he's suggesting to chill for a while, take in the sights. Your gift is your intelligence and power of mind, but it can also be a shadow that makes for inefficiency. Focus your thoughts on what you want to manifest, and (as you've so amply demonstrated!) it will be so." She wrote back and said it was right on the money.

You can do the same by simply observing those animals that come to you in any of the ways mentioned above. Use your imagination and allow Spirit to communicate through the wonderful avenues that our animal brothers and sisters provide.

CHAPTER 10

THE GRASSHOPPER SINGS: "LET THE SONG FIND YOU"

Rock and roll fantasies

I got my first guitar when I was sixteen. I learned some chords, some finger-picking, a few folk songs, and some tunes by some of my favorites, including Dylan, Neil Young, James Taylor and others. Playing guitar and singing became a part of my life and has continued to be so up until this day.

In the eighties, a friend and I who played together frequently wrote some songs, went into a recording studio and put them down on tape. We also performed in a few places and even had a band for a short while, but the rock and roll fantasy faded with age and the distractions inherent in trying to be a responsible adult. And in retrospect, most of these early tunes we crafted weren't all that good. Although I continued to play guitar and sing off and on for the next several years, I figured that the songwriting and performing was just a phase that had passed, never to be revisited.

Wrong.

Something took hold of me a couple of years ago. I rewrote a couple of those older songs and started writing new ones, increasingly caught up in a delightful fever of lyrical and musical creativity. Before long I had several songs in finalized form. I felt a passion for composing and playing these tunes. I wanted them to express something meaningful and hopefully stir something in anyone who listened. I felt like I was transcribing them, that they were inspired and guided by some other force, and I was the vehicle through which the songs showed up. I played them for my wife and friends and in a couple of coffee houses and got a very positive response. Everyone encouraged me to get them recorded.

So eventually I did some home recording, but realized I needed to go to a professional recording studio to get the quality I wanted. Since I hadn't been in a recording studio for years, I was nervous about it, but in spite of my trepidation, I made an appointment with someone close to our house and set up a recording date for the following day.

Grasshopper's message

I was sitting in my office the afternoon before the next day's appointment at the recording studio, enjoying the fair weather and the slight breeze coming in from the open sliding-glass doors, feeling a mixture of nervousness and excitement, organizing my songs in preparation for recording them. The critical voice of the ego kept popping in and out, saying such things as "What do you think you're doing? Who do you think you are?" as if warning me, like

Robot in the old series, *Lost in Space*, saying, "Danger! Danger, Will Robinson!" It's interesting how when we stretch our comfort zone there's typically a part of us that wants us to remain safe and not take risks. But always opting for safety and comfort is a sort of death in itself, isn't it?

As I was contemplating all this, a huge grasshopper jumped from outside and landed squarely just to the right of my computer. I hadn't seen any grasshoppers for years, and here was one plopped down right by me! As I stared at this . . . this being for a few moments, I thought, "Okay, Mr. Spirit Animal Guy, what does 'Grasshopper' mean?" The message was "Take the leap!" But I wanted more. I first looked in my book, *Animal Spirit Guides,* but lo and behold! Nothing about Grasshopper! Okay, Steven, let's do what you tell others to do, and do some research.[3]

I jumped on the internet, did a search for "Grasshopper totem," "Grasshopper spirit animal," and "Grasshopper animal spirit guide." In most of the sites I came across, Grasshopper was noted for presenting itself to musicians and other artists, and as well was being an animal of song and dance. Others referred to Grass-hopper's song as being a muse and inspiring creativity. Still others referred to Grasshopper as having the gift of the power of song, noting the ancient belief that song has the power to alter consciousness and communicate with animal and spirit relationships.

---

3 Adapted from, Steven Farmer's website, *Earth Magic*, "The Grasshopper Sings 'Let the Song Find You'," <http://www.earthmagic.net/shamanic-journey/the-grasshopper-sings-let-the-song-find-you/> viewed March 13, 2017.

Okay, okay! Chills ran up and down my spine as I read this. I once heard that when you get chills or the hairs on the back of your neck stick up, either you're getting sick or having a spiritual experience. Wasn't sick, so must have been a spiritual experience. I much prefer these kinds of messages from spirit guides, the ones that hit you right between the eyes and where the message is obvious. I couldn't back out of this one even if I wanted to!

I'm happy to report that I did get to the studio the next day and that I recorded five basic tracks (guitar and vocals) of my songs. I was pleased with the results and it confirmed my intention to later create a CD, so stay tuned . . .

Oh, yeah—one more thing. Recently I was working on a new song and was struggling to find the right music for the lyrics that had flowed out of my pen. I played it one way, then another, not finding the right tune, and I was getting frustrated. I decided to call on Grasshopper spirit. When I did, I heard very clearly, "Let the song find you."

And it did.

CHAPTER 11

WHY DID THE TORTOISE CROSS THE ROAD?

The road

had journeyed across the country from Los Angeles to upstate New York to present a workshop at the Omega Institute about connecting with the spirit world. After a five-hour flight and two-and-a-half-hour drive, I parked at the B and B to unload my luggage and rest for a few moments, then hopped in the car and drove the few miles to the nearby town of Rhinebeck. I wanted to gather some supplies for my three-day stay, and from my previous visits, knew of an outstanding health food store in the village that had many of my favorite goods.

As I was driving along the somewhat twisty road on this unseasonably hot and humid day, appreciating the forested panorama on either side, I noticed another driver fast approaching from behind. I gripped the wheel tighter as he approached. The car came within a car's length as I snaked my way along the bendy road at forty miles per hour, with no place to pull over or for the other car to pass. I slowed a bit, thinking the other driver might pass in spite of the double yellow lines. My attention was divided between the road ahead and the vehicle in the rear view mirror that seemed to be attached by an invisible cord to my car.

Suddenly I caught something on the pavement, some small, indistinct movement just ahead. It was a tortoise that was crossing the road! He had just crossed the dividing line moving from left to right, moseying along—naturally—at a tortoise pace, clearly directed to be on the other side of the road. All in the blink of an eye, I swerved and gratefully avoided running over this beautiful creature. But what about the car behind me? Immediately I glanced in the rear view mirror, and to my great relief saw that the driver had also managed to avoid hitting the tortoise.

Once I had gotten through the initial shock of the situation I realized that my little friend was still in danger, so I did a U-turn and tracked back to the scene of the crossing. When I arrived, there was a yellow Volkswagen Beetle parked off to the side of the road. A woman was escorting the tortoise by standing behind him, shepherding him for the brief remainder of his trek by walking behind. Occasionally she would clap her hands, prompting the tortoise to scoot along a bit faster for at least a couple of steps. I breathed a sigh of relief, thanked the woman for caring so much, and continued on my journey to Rhinebeck.

The message

When you experience an unusual sighting of an animal like this, it's bringing you a message from Spirit. In order to decipher the message, close your eyes, take a couple of deep breaths, see that animal in your mind's eye, and silently ask what message they have for you. Once you've asked, pay attention to whatever shows up next, whether through images, words, sensations, thoughts, or some combination of these. The communication may be very clear, or may be somewhat cryptic or dreamlike, but however it shows up, this is your answer.

With the tortoise who crossed the road, given that I was driving, I obviously couldn't shut my eyes. Instead, I just let it work me, asking the spirit of Tortoise what message he was trying to give me. The communication came through gradually over the next several hours, and consisted of some very simple messages that proved valuable not only for the class I was about to teach, but also every area of my life.

Here's a summary of the message:

> SLOW DOWN! You've got all the time in the world. Be willing to stick your neck out, take some risks. You are protected and cared for, and you can always retreat if necessary. Know that help is always nearby when you need it—just put the word out. It will often show up in unexpected and surprising ways.

This was helpful for me since I had started doing random power animal readings, by tuning into someone's animal spirit guide and relaying what the spirit guide was communicating. Tortoise encouraged me to go for it, to not hold back, to trust the information I get and pass it along to the individual I was reading. His shell was a reminder that protection was always available.

I went on to teach the class and throughout, Tortoise's message continued to play itself out in many ways. My readings were sharp and detailed, thanks to the willingness on the part of the animal spirits to show themselves to me so clearly. Tortoise reminded me that I was safe at all times, in spite of the things of life whizzing by me, just like the cars whizzing by our friend on the road.

CHAPTER 12

ANIMAL SPIRIT GUIDES AND ANCESTORS

**(excerpt from *Healing Ancestral Karma*
by Dr. Steven Farmer)**

Spirit is communicating with us all the time in so many different ways, especially in the visible and tangible realm of the natural world. Picking up on the messages is a matter of learning to listen to and interpret those communications, much like our ancient ancestors knew how to do. For them, paying attention to signs from the natural world was often a matter of survival, yet for us in the modern world we have largely forgotten how to do so.

One of the most accessible ways to receive messages from the natural world is through the animals that show up at times to bring us a message from Spirit. Every time an animal shows up it doesn't necessarily mean that it's a message from Spirit, however when an animal shows up in an unusual way or repeatedly in a short period of time, it is most likely delivering a message. It can be the physical animal or a symbol of the animal, such as in dreams, billboards, television programs, or even the persistent thought of a particular animal. It's like your very own psychic reading. When your consciousness stays attuned to the possibility of messages from a spirit animal that is an aspect of the physical being, you're more likely to receive messages.

For instance, I was working with a client recently, did some readings with my *Earth Magic Oracle Cards* and one clear message from the reading was that she was going through a major transformation. Even coming to see me at the recommendation of a friend was a bit of a stretch for her as she had never been exposed to shamanic work, let alone psychic/intuitive readings. She was very enthused and found that the reading really resonated with her, indicating she could tell her life was about to change, as she said, "Big time!"

When she walked out my office door, there to greet her was a butterfly flitting in, out, and around the bushes. I had told her briefly about animal spirit guides in the session, so as I stood at the doorway observing this beautiful creature and its elegant dance, I commented, "There! A butterfly is often a message to 'get ready for big changes.' A major transformation is underway." She smiled brightly and thanked both the butterfly and me for this confirmation from a spirit animal!

When it comes to ancestors, there are a couple of instances you can tell that it's a message sent from an ancestor. If the animal was a favorite one of your ancestors, such as your grandfather, and if that animal shows up in physical form and/or symbolic form, even if only repetitive thoughts about it, it's sending a message from him. Typically it's at least a reminder that he's doing okay in the afterlife.

Another common occurrence is one that happens shortly before or following the death of a loved one. I've heard quite a few stories of an animal showing up soon after. A woman we'll call Patty lost her beloved grandmother to whom she was very close. She was sitting on her patio the next day following the funeral and a dove alighted on the table. She looked at this dove and something in her *knew* that her grandmother had sent this precious little being. It reassured her that Grandma was doing all right. That dove did the same thing the next three days, landing on the patio table when Patty was seated there. After the fourth visit, the dove was rarely seen except for occasional visits.[4]

4 Farmer, Steven, *Healing Ancestral Karma*, Hierophant Publishing, San Antonio, 2014.

CHAPTER 13

COOPER'S HAWK

**(excerpt from *Healing Ancestral Karma*
by Dr. Steven Farmer)**

I met Dan and Sara Beaupre at a workshop and they had a heart-rending and inspiring story to relate about an animal messenger from their son who died when he was four years old. They agreed to write out the story and it is used with their permission:

Our life was simple, filled with nothing but pure joy and love. All three of us—my wife Sara, our son Cooper, and myself, Dan—loved the outdoors and have always felt very connected to Mother Earth. On April 13, 2011 our life drastically changed for the worst. Without warning, we would have to endure the greatest pain of our lifetime. Our son Cooper tragically lost his life in a terrible accident. A forbidden woodpile tumbled onto him and ultimately claim his life force.

We had never really put much thought into the spirit world or "the other side" yet we never discounted it either. At that time our faith in God had completely vanished. We were swept away in our grief, trying to adapt to a life without our only son. Over time we met several people who introduced us to a whole new way of looking at life and encouraged us to seek answers. We were desperate to find our son on the other side! We vowed that if we could not have him in the physical world, we would do absolutely anything in our power to connect with him in the spirit world.

And thus our journey began! Our faith in God, Spirit, the other side, or whatever you want call it would return to us but not nearly in the way we would have expected. We were taught to open our minds and hearts and welcome the soul of our child into our lives. We began our journey experiencing undeniable signs from Cooper. As we grew together spiritually we began to find our way living life the best way we knew how. Our perception on life changed dramatically and we welcomed it.

In August of 2011, about four months after Cooper's transition, I was driving home from work and I couldn't get Cooper off my mind. This wasn't unusual as I talked to my son every chance I got. This particular day I was feeling a bit disconnected, lonely for my son. I graciously asked Cooper to please send us a sign to let us know that his spirit is near and that he is with me.

As I drove in my driveway, I was shocked to see a beautiful animal awaiting my arrival. I stopped my truck in complete amazement. Standing there before me was a full grown red-tailed hawk. I got out of my truck and something told me to sit down and extend my hand to the bird. So I did! At that time, the hawk started to walk toward me and sat just inches from my hand. I couldn't believe my eyes, that this extraordinary event was taking place before me! I was most certainly not afraid of him and he was not afraid of me. We were just two souls sitting on a gravel driveway staring at each other in complete amazement.

I suddenly realized that I needed a camera, as nobody would believe me that this was actually happening. I carefully got up and grabbed my phone out of my truck. I called Sara and told her to come to the end of the driveway so she could witness what was happening and then I took a whole bunch of photos. As I was waiting for Sara I thought to myself, either this hawk was injured or else it had prey nearby. I didn't understand the power of this bird, much less the gift it was bringing to our family, until later.

As Sara approached the hawk flew into a tree. Of course Sara was blown away by its beauty and kept saying this was a huge sign. There was absolutely no way a red-tailed hawk is going to let you get that close to it. Then Sara said, "We have that book that talks about the spirit of animals and what they represent!" We ran back to our house and paged through the book as fast as we could, and what we discovered nearly knocked us off our feet.

A red tail hawk is a messenger and is also referred to as a Cooper's hawk. Looking at each other with utter amazement, we immediately understood the connection: it was our son's way of communicating with us. He was bringing us a special message. We realized at that moment that our family was receiving one of life's greatest gifts from our beloved Cooper.

The serendipity of asking for a sign and it appearing as a Cooper's hawk was undeniable! Cooper was so clever to use an animal such as a Cooper's hawk to get our attention. The hawk stayed around our home for a total of five days. All of our family members got to come in contact with the hawk. After the very last family member saw him, the hawk moved on.

For the two of us, the hawk was one of the greatest gifts Cooper could have ever given us. We will forever be thankful to feel the energy of our baby once again through the spirit of a red-tailed hawk. Spirit is real and palpable. Sara now practices Mediumship to help others heal their hearts from the trauma of losing a loved one. I continue to hold the spirit of my son close to my heart. For a time in my life I didn't believe, but now I can never deny.

In October of 2013, I received the gift once again. As I was cleaning up outside on a rainy day, to my surprise I looked up and there he was: a beautiful red-tailed hawk. At first the hawk startled me but I instantly knew there was a another big message he was delivering. Sara and I sat inches from the hawk and it literally followed me around my house just like Cooper did when he was physically present. Playing fearlessly and trusting our every move, the hawk stayed for three days this time.

We're so incredibly grateful that this transpired and that Cooper continues to be so present in our lives. We're grateful that we never closed the door on our son's spirit.

In these situations where a deceased loved one as ancestor is trying to reach you, birds (such as the hawk in the above story) and butterflies seem to be the most common, though a friend of mine noticed a dolphin swam close to shore right alongside her as she walked along the beach following her father's death. It isn't that the animal visits is your deceased loved one, but is definitely a messenger or courier. Though it may be more extensive, the message is usually quite simple and straightforward—that they are doing okay. After all, they don't have a body to contend with—at least until their soul chooses to incarnate again.[5]

5 Farmer, Steven, *Healing Ancestral Karma*, Hierophant Publishing, San Antonio, 2014.

CHAPTER 14

THE ARTIST AND
THE SNAKE

You either love them or hate/fear them, but what can't be denied is that snakes are embedded deeply in our consciousness, a powerful spiritual reality and symbol of major transformation. People that have never seen a snake will dream of them. In some traditions if you're bitten by a highly poisonous snake and survive, you're considered to be a powerful healer. The American Medical Association has two intertwined snakes as part of their caduceus, and Hermes carried a snake as a symbol. Kundalini yoga works with the energies along the spine that can be likened to a serpent and is sometimes portrayed as such. Jeremy Narby in one of my favorite books, *The Cosmic Serpent,* proposes that DNA is often represented in indigenous traditions and art as two intertwined serpents. There is a richness to the physical and spiritual stories with Snake, snake energy, and Snake medicine.

A friend of mine, Paul Huessenstamm, who does this amazing spiritual/visionary art (www.mandalas.com), recently had an experience with Snake medicine. I invited him to contribute this dramatic story, for which he granted permission as an illustration of how potent this particular power animal can be:

Snake dream

"I've been painting pictures for several years now that I know have been inspired by Spirit/God/Source; a whole range of images from mandalas to deities from various religions and devotional practices. I've also traveled extensively throughout the world continuously over the past few years to give painting workshops, with the intention of helping others tap into that inspirational source for their creations. Although I've been making a decent living as an artist, the greater success that I felt was in my destiny remained elusive—until recent events that were foreshadowed by a dream I had in September of 2005.

"It was a very powerful Snake dream that, as it turned out, predicted subsequent events in my life. In fact, I added this dream to my dream deck, a collection of about twenty-five 'big dreams' I've collected over the years, each of which I've written out on a card to carry with me wherever I go. Many of them have foretold and predicted significant events in my life.

"It was quite a complex dream, and one of the most significant parts was at the end of the dream. I was in a room with cobras all around me, like in *Raiders of the Lost Ark*, and although I loved snakes, I knew these ones were poisonous. I fell onto my belly and one of the cobras bit my bare foot. I woke up in the dream (lucid dreaming) and said to myself, 'I'm going to die.' I felt the poison going in me, but instead of killing me, I felt elated as the poison surged into my system. When I stood up, instead of snakes there were now a bunch of people around me, and I was feeling ecstatic, full of life and vitality.

"I knew that Snake represented transformation, so I figured the dream signified the start of a process of deep transformation. Being hit by a cobra you'd expect to be sick and possibly die, not exhilarated, but this dream led to greater wholeness, not death. Based on my history with dreams, I knew that it was predicting some significant change in my life. I just didn't know what it would be."

Snake medicine

"It was now five months later. I'd been traveling in southern China for nearly three weeks doing my painting workshops. When they concluded, I flew to meet up with my wife Amana at our beach house we'd rented in Bali, and was very much looking forward to a break and to spending time with her there. I got to Bali, spent the night, had a wonderful breakfast, and then went surfing. The waves were perfect, the sun was out, and from the water I could see a number of the temples that are so prevalent in Bali. Life was perfect and I couldn't have been any happier. After surfing I had a light lunch and jumped in the shower.

"Unbeknownst to me, there was a snake in the back part of the shower. As I stepped from the shower, before realizing the snake was there, I felt a sudden bolt of lightning in my body. This small, black snake had sunk his two fangs deep into my little toe. For the next few moments I went into one of those altered states where your whole life goes racing through your mind. I was thinking, 'So this is how it ends. Being bitten by a poisonous snake in Bali.' I'd been told that when snakes had fangs they were usually poisonous. As I screamed, I somehow knew that I wasn't the only one that had been bitten. Amana was in the other room and I knew that she'd been bitten also.

"A Balinese man came into our home and we asked him if the snake was poisonous. He said that all snakes in Bali were very bad and we should go right to the hospital, so we hopped in the car and for the next hour we battled a lot of traffic and interruptions to get to the hospital in the nearest village.

"As we headed toward the hospital, the dream came back to me. I started to question God. 'C'mon, don't throw me a twist where this snake really was poisonous and I die!' My heart was racing, but since I didn't have any other symptoms it was probably anxiety. I was actually laughing as to how being bitten by a snake in Bali would end it.

"The village hospital didn't have the proper facilities, so they put both of us in an ambulance that took us downtown where there was a much larger hospital. There they gave us all sorts of shots, and like my dream, there were all sorts of people around me. I was hoping they'd give me the anti-venom, but an American nurse who'd lived in Bali and had helped a lot of people said they would only give me the anti-venom if my symptoms started to become severe. Otherwise I'd be sick for a couple of weeks.

"After a rather noisy and disturbing overnight stay, the next morning we both seemed okay so we checked out and went home. We spent the next three weeks in Bali, which gave me time to not only rest and recover but also contemplate this experience. That's when it hit me that the dream was exactly right—some big changes were afoot.

"I loved my work, but knew I'd been traveling far too much, so I made a big decision to cancel all my trips and workshops and clear my calendar for the next three months. Ordinarily I would have been traveling somewhere every couple of weeks, but I just wanted to stay at home and didn't want to go to any foreign countries."

Breakthrough

"After a couple weeks I got a call from someone at Agape, a very large and well-known New Age church in Los Angeles headed by Michael Beckwith. I was invited to put up several of my paintings in the sanctuary at Agape and leave them there for at least the next six months, which would expose them to the thousands of spiritually minded people that attend their services and related activities every week. I had ninety days to prepare for the biggest show of my life, which meant I'd have to not only prepare my existing pieces but also create some new pieces for the show.

"About a month later, I suddenly realized that this little snake and the associated Snake medicine had been a part of putting this all together. Even though I thought I was dying, it really marked the beginning of an ecstatic transformation into a whole new level of my work. It would be much more in the public eye, particularly to others who would undoubtedly resonate with it.

"I thought, 'God, that little snake was one of my greatest

allies.' Had that little guy not bitten me, I'd have been too busy to do the Agape show. That snakebite was one of the most positive things that ever happened to me as an artist."

CHAPTER 15

ANIMAL SPIRIT GUIDES AND SCUBA DIVING

Scuba diving was always something that other people did, so I had never given it much thought. Several years ago, while on a cruise through the islands of Tahiti, I decided to give it a go in the warm waters of Bora Bora. I must confess that one of the reasons was to be able to say, "My first scuba dive was at Bora Bora." Bragging rights. I enjoyed my first diving experience, right up until my air ran out—which happened within a few minutes—when I had to use the secondary breather on the instructor's apparatus.

Second dive off of Moorea, I had a panic episode. I was able to breathe through it and it did pass, but it planted itself in my mind and body memory. Two other dives some time later resulted in first not having enough weights on, so my guide had to tether me to himself to keep me down, and on the next dive I received a bruised eardrum from floating up and down too quickly because I gamely tried to adjust everything so I could stay at one level. I decided after this last experience that scuba diving was just not for me.

Less than a year later, I set up a vacation trip to Kona, Hawaii, one of my favorite places to visit. I expected to see some friends there, particularly Duke and Angie, who were dedicated divers. Of course, when I checked with them, they wanted go diving and asked if I would go with them. I reflexively said "Sure" and plans were put into motion, one of them being a boat dive with Angie and Duke scheduled a few days after I was to arrive. Even though I'd agreed, I remained non-committal and very skeptical that I would do anything that would involve more than wearing a mask, fins, and a snorkel (which I'd enjoyed on a number of occasions previously).

I realized as I approached the date of my flight to Hawaii that I was highly ambivalent about the prospect of scuba diving, but I had already agreed to do so. On the one hand, the warrior in me was urging me on, telling me to take a chance and view it as an adventure. On the other, memories of all the bad parts of my previous experiences made my stomach tighten and my throat clutch up. My first four dives weren't exactly catastrophes but they were, shall we say, challenging.

As I sat at my desk considering all this, I turned and looked at the deck of my *Power Animal Oracle Cards* that had arrived only two days before. Hmmm. Why don't I just check out what they have to say? I had only tested them out by doing readings with a couple of friends, and they had been surprisingly accurate. Why not ask the question about scuba diving! So I did.

I got still, silently asked the question, then pulled a card. Since they were new, another card stuck to the one I'd pulled, which meant that both cards were part of the reading. I took a deep breath, part of me hoping to find Turtle on the other side telling me to retreat. Instead, there was the statement at the bottom of Elephant: "You will overcome any obstacles."

Hmm. Okay. Now for the next. As I peeled the Elephant card from the other, the words at the bottom jumped out at me: "Just do it!" Beaver had spoken. Although appreciative of such straightforward and direct advice from these cards that the animal spirits and I had co-created, I was in a bit of shock. I knew what I had to do: go scuba diving.

After I worked a bit more on my next book, *Animal Spirit Guides,* played my guitar a while, then went to the kitchen to get a snack. I was pondering the messages I had just received, still dancing in my mind with the thought of taking the plunge—no pun intended. A few days later I made it to Hawaii. Since I still had a considerable amount to do on my book, I remained at the hotel for the first four days of the vacation, furiously writing away, knowing that destiny was awaiting me on a boat from Jack's Diving Locker.

I finally reached a place in the book where I could take a break. The day of reckoning came. We went out on the boat and with Jeff, the owner of Jack's Diving Locker, as my trusted guide, I did my first dive of the day. I figured I would do at least two dives that day to satisfy the "suggestions" I'd received from Elephant and Beaver, and these would be the clincher: either I'd hang up my tank after that, or perhaps decide to do this from time to time. Though I'd received excellent coaching from Jeff, the first dive was more of an "at least I did it" type of dive. I can't honestly say I enjoyed it, although there were some pretty remarkable sights, but afterwards I wasn't sure I wanted to do another.

However, the advice I'd gotten from the spirit animals continued to echo in my head. So I did a second dive, which was actually—well—enjoyable. I finally understood how to negotiate the buoyancy factor, keeping myself at a particular level. It struck me that there was an entirely different world under the sea, one populated by all these alien creatures, yet still part of this remarkable planet. And a way to view it was doing exactly what we were doing, by donning these underwater space suits and breathing air from a tank strapped to our backs.

Later that evening I went out to sit by the ocean and meditate. One of my favorite quotes came to me, by Chief Dan George:

> *If you talk with the animals they will talk with you, and you will know each other. If you do not talk to them, you will not know them, and what you do not know, you will fear. What one fears one destroys.*

In my meditation Whale spirit came to me and gave me the message as follows:

> *Your assignment is to show others how to talk with the animals. Let people know that the communication won't be like in Dr. Doolittle, but instead it is a communication with the spirit of that animal, or it is a communication with the essence of the entire species of that particular*

animal represented by one member. When you do so there's an exchange that takes place.

The reason Spirit conveyed the message through Elephant and Beaver to go scuba diving is because you were out of balance. Your energy and power is too dense at times, because you are such a strong earth sign [I'm a triple-earth sign]. By being in the water from time to time in this way will bring a greater power and balance. This helps you honor and fulfill the need to touch the earth in more ways than sitting on a rock or walking along the beach.

This kingdom of the sea is not the usual earth you know. It's a different world, yet it's still Earth when you incorporate all the elements we experience here as sentient beings. You know in your heart of hearts that you're intimately associated with and related to all sentient beings, who are truly your brothers and sisters. And yes, lobsters do feel pain. But then, most everybody does at first when they die. The pain passes. Yet you can feel the pain of any beings if you simply pay attention.

I spent a few more days on the Big Island and did two more dives. I doubt that I'll ever have an intense passion for scuba diving, but during these dives I felt a much greater appreciation for these seemingly alien life forms that exist there, knowing that they too are part of this wondrous web of life that exists here on this beautiful earth.

CHAPTER 16

HAWK PAYS
A VISIT

I was just getting out of bed when I caught a flutter of wings out of the corner of my eye. I watched as all of the birds that had been feeding outside the bedroom window scattered. It's not unusual to see doves and a smattering of other birds on the deck and in the tree just outside, as I often left birdseed there just for that purpose. When they're alarmed by something, they typically fly off, so I was curious as to what had caused this ruckus. Perched on one of the branches a few feet away was a magnificent red-tailed hawk, solemnly gazing about, surveying his kingdom, supremely confident and poised, awaiting some instinctual signal for his next move.

I'd seen this particular hawk on a few occasions, but it had been several months since his last visit. Since Hawk has been a consistently profound and accurate messenger, I asked Hawk spirit the meaning of this visitation. What I heard was, "Stay focused and don't get distracted. Keep things in perspective." Straightforward and simple—not cryptic or abstract at all. That's the way I like my messages from Spirit—whoever the spirit messenger is.

Given that I was working on a new product—specifically the *Messages from Your Animal Spirit Guides Oracle Cards*—and the manuscript was due in just five short weeks, I appreciated this counsel from Hawk. It takes discipline to write, and I confess that it's sometimes easier to enjoy computer games such as *Backgammon* or *Solitaire*. Not at all productive, but they're mindless and make excellent diversions. I'd highly recommend them if you ever want pointless distractions from accomplishing your purpose. Of course, they don't contribute to getting any more writing accomplished—and the deadline was quickly approaching. I knew this is what Hawk had in mind when he communicated his message to me.

So that morning I sat down at my computer and diligently began writing. That lasted about fifteen minutes, at which point I decided to check my email. Yes, another diversion that could have easily waited. However when I clicked the button to access my email account, nothing happened! The internet wasn't working! Suddenly I panicked, feeling as if this was a crisis of immense proportions.

I spent the next two and a half hours on the phone with our internet company and with the Apple computer service center, trying this and that, with no success, growing increasingly frustrated, doing a lot of muttering and clenching my fists and my gut. I had set a goal that morning after Hawk's visit to get a specific amount of writing accomplished, and now this seemingly urgent matter had come up to delay my mission.

Just when I felt like throwing things, suddenly the internet and wireless were operating like they were supposed to.

I was relieved and grateful. I immediately went online to check my email. It was the day before Christmas, so there was hardly any email at all, the only interesting one being from a guy in Nigeria that wanted me to help him out by transferring several million dollars into my account, for which I'd get a percentage. Hmm. Slightly tempting but seemed a little too risky.

I furrowed my brow, trying to remember why it had been so critical that I go online and check my email in the first place, but for the life of me, I couldn't remember. Whatever had been my reason at the time, it was lost to what had seemed to be a matter of grave importance—getting the internet working again. It was then I once again heard Hawk's message: "Stay focused and don't get distracted. Keep things in perspective."

I laughed out loud at my follies. I had completely forgotten to apply Hawk's beautiful and purposeful message; I had created an entire drama around a very minor dilemma! Fixing the internet could have easily waited, but instead became a convenient diversion from my writing. I tricked myself into thinking it was a crisis, subconsciously undermining my intention at that time to stay focused. Oh, well—joke's on me. Maybe Coyote was around, working his trickster medicine.

I diligently continued writing my book each day. I dumped the *Solitaire* game, but *Backgammon* still had a bit of a hold on me. About a week later, guess who appeared once again in the tree outside our window? You got it. The hawk. A gentle nudge from Hawk to stay focused. Okay. Stay focused, don't get distracted, keep writing and be aware of what I put out. Strong messages highlighted by the second visitation from Hawk.

And as if that wasn't enough, just to make sure I got the message, about two weeks after the second visit from Hawk, he showed up again! Although I was on a deadline, I confess that I was still occasionally goofing off and playing *Backgammon* on the computer. Out of the corner of my eye I again saw a flurry of feathers and motion—this time just a few feet away inside the house! The hawk was between my desk and the closed sliding-glass door that faces the backyard.

I got up, walked around to the front of my desk, and there was that same hawk I'd seen before, shaking and flailing away at the glass with his wings and talons, trying to make a quick exit. I spoke calmly to him, as it was obvious he was terrified. After a couple of minutes, I opened the sliding-glass door and the hawk flew out, shaken but not injured. Okay, third reminder. Got it!

As I turned to go back to my desk and of course, focus on my project, I spotted a dove tucked away between the desk and the printer, who exited very quickly through the open door as soon as there was an opportunity. Putting this all together, I realized that the hawk had been chasing after the dove and both had flown in through the open doors at the front of the house, down the hallway, and into my office at the back of the house. So Hawk in this third visit was a gigantic exclamation point for the previous messages.

An additional message that came to me from Hawk was to pursue the goal (of completing the work on the oracle cards) with relentless focus and diligence, no matter what happens. Dove's message was twofold. First, that there will be a happy outcome, and second, to be as peaceful and calm throughout the process, in spite of any disturbances.

I'm happy to say I was able to finish the oracle cards and turn them in on the deadline. Thank you Hawk! Thank you Dove!

CHAPTER 17

'AUMAKUA, FAMILIARS, AND SPIRIT ANIMALS ... OH MY!!!

Animals and spirit animals

From the Rainbow Serpent of the Aborigines of Australia that birthed the land and its inhabitants, to the Cowardly Lion that accompanied Dorothy to Oz, to the tale you tell of the hummingbird that hovered for several seconds two feet from your nose, cultural and personal stories and mythologies are rampant with animals and spirit animals. These stories and experiences resonate with our instinctual connection to the animal kingdom, as well as conveying an innate kinship with this vast realm of beings with whom we share our planet. We owe a great deal of thanks to our animal brothers and sisters, who give so much to us humans, such as companionship, warmth, and food. In some traditions it's even told that humans descended from the animals.

As for animal spirit guides, the awareness that Spirit

sometimes shows up in animal form was inherent in the cultural beliefs of indigenous peoples. These traditions all have some variations depending on the particular culture, but the common thread is the unquestionable acceptance of animals as spirit guides. Even some creation myths credit spirit animals with the birth of the world, such as the Rainbow Serpent as mentioned above.

As human consciousness continues to evolve during this present era, we look with greater interest and curiosity at what these ancient peoples can teach us. Some of the greatest lessons are what we can learn from the animals, whether in the flesh or in spirit.

When an animal makes an appearance (whether physically or symbolically) in an unusual way or repeatedly in a short span of time, the spirit of that animal is attempting to get a message to you. Often you'll have a hunch or a sense of the message from this spirit guide. Trust it. As you'll see, it might even be an ancestor: a distant, long-deceased relative that is guiding and protecting you by showing up in animal form.

'Aumakua

Every culture has a slightly different take on the idea of animal spirit guides. From ancient Hawaiian spirituality, still alive today, comes the concept of *'aumakua*—spirit guides clothed in the language, customs, and stories of this culture.

'Aumakua (ow-ma-koo-ah) are the spirits of biological and spiritual ancestors. They can be called on for protection, guidance, and spiritual support. The very first 'aumakua were the children of humans who had mated with the *Akua,* or primary gods, the main ones being Ku (Koo), Kane (Kah-nay), Lono, and Kanaloa (Kah-nah-low-ah). When someone died, they went through a period of time where they stayed with these Akua and thereby acquired a degree of mana, or power. Eventually they could make themselves known to their descendants. One of the most prevalent ways they could make their appearance—although not limited to this—was through animals and animal spirits. They could also show up in the wind, rain, or lightning, or in your dreams.

Many people have reported experiences similar to the concept of 'aumakua, where an ancestor has come to them in the form of an animal. For instance, after her mother's death, Julie had frequent visitations from hummingbirds. They would sometimes hover directly in front of her as if to say, "Look at me!" Her mother loved hummingbirds as did Julie, and Julie felt certain that this little being was a messenger from her mother to let her know that she was okay. Hummingbird is Julie's 'aumakua.

Familiars

From a few centuries ago in Western Europe, similar to the Hawaiian 'aumakua, comes the idea of *familiars.* During the Middle Ages, familiars were mainly associated with witches, while these days they're associated with Wiccans. Familiars are spirits often showing up as animals, although they can also inhabit objects, such as rings or lockets. The spirit animal can also be the companion of magicians and sorcerers. Think Harry Potter's owl.

Another term for familiars that has been grossly distorted over the centuries is *daemon* or *demon.* Up until the persecution of witches that began in late thirteenth century, the word itself did not mean something evil. In other words, the word demon got, well, demonized. In more contemporary terms, a demon would simply be an animal spirit guide or power animal, often embodied in a companion animal such as a cat or dog. In fact, older women who kept a cat during the persecutions were often accused of being witches and put to death, whether or not they actually practiced witchcraft.

An animal spirit guide by any other name, whether called 'aumakua, a familiar, a power animal, or a totem animal, is still an animal spirit guide. And they can help you navigate through this lifetime. And who knows—maybe the next time you spot that hummingbird, it just might be Great-grandma Jane telling you that she's watching over you, so know you're safe and protected—and while you're at it, lighten up!

CHAPTER 18

WHAT DID THE ANIMALS KNOW?: instinct, survival, and the tsunami

(written after the tsunami of 2004)

Even though in the recent tsunami there was a tremendous loss of human life, many beings survived, both human and animal whether by fortune, circumstances, or innate intelligence. We savor such stories, such as the man that was adrift for days in the ocean, clinging to a floating tree. What also caught my eye were the stories about the animals. Amongst the countless bodies of humans, not one dead animal was found. Most, if not all, of the animals that were near the coast had somehow been alerted to the danger and left for the higher ground.

There were several reports of animals reacting before the tsunami hit. Antelopes were seen running to a nearby hilltop. Elephants, leopards, deer and other wild animals in a national park survived the massive wave by escaping and running to higher ground. Elephants that gave tourists rides became very agitated a few minutes before the tsunami hit and lumbered up the hillside, some with tourists still on their backs!

How did the animals know? What signals alerted them? And what can we learn from the animals and their life-saving behavior?

A few theories have been proposed, particularly ideas that the animals were responding to a "sixth sense." Yet this sixth sense could more accurately be called a "first" or "primary" sense, something that closely guides and determines much of the behavior of all animals. This primary sense is instinct, a product of the reptilian brain, that primitive part of the brain that's in every species of animal (including the human animal), bird, or reptile.

This reptilian or "lower" brain is what governs our basic survival functions, such as breathing, heart rate, reproductive drive, and so forth. It's also responsible for alerting us to potentially life-threatening danger. When you have a gut feeling, this is instinct operating. Sensations in your body are warning you of some sort of danger, and it's quite natural to either fight or flee, yet most of us have learned to largely ignore these signals from the body that are warning us of danger.

Much of this ignorance of instinct is due to a number of factors. First, we're conditioned to disregard these signals, starting with our childhood upbringing. You can't very well fight or run when you're little and you're threatened by the very adult caregivers you depend on for your survival. Instead you learn to freeze in reaction to a tormenting adult, and this can become a generalized and habitual response to other potential dangers. While this may have been adaptive in childhood, it doesn't necessarily serve us when carried over into adulthood. In addition, we learn to shut down our senses and become somewhat numb, disregarding bodily cues to possible threats.

Another reason is that we fear losing control. It doesn't look very dignified to be running for the hills when there's no obvious danger, even though your gut may be telling you otherwise. The rational mind learns to override these instinctual urgings, attempting to provide a false sense of safety. Lastly and perhaps most importantly, we have to one degree or another become removed from the natural world, shielded from the earth's rhythms and seasons by the trappings of civilization.

Yet there are stories of some groups of people who were more attuned to the natural world and, much like the animals, listened to their instincts and the environmental cues of the impending disaster. Some tribal peoples in India and Thailand managed to escape the tidal waves completely. All 250 members of the Jarawa tribe in India, a tribe that spans back 70,000 years and still retains its indigenous roots, fled into the jungle and remained there for several days. Government officials and anthropologists believe that ancient knowledge of the movement of the wind, sea, and birds may have saved them and other tribal peoples from the tsunami.

In another instance, a group of Thai fishermen known as the Morgan sea gypsies saved an entire village of 181 people because of their knowledge of the ocean and its currents that had been passed down from generation to generation. Unlike some of the Thais who headed to the beach to pick up flapping fish left on the sand when the sea drained out of the beaches, the sea gypsies headed for a temple in the mountains.

The vast majority of the people in these regions were apparently not attuned to the environmental and internal physical cues that foretold of the coming tsunami. Even with the veneer of contemporary conditioning we respond quickly to those dangers that are immediate and apparent to our senses. However, the signs of the looming catastrophe were less obvious, so in spite of the massive earthquake, for most there was no reason to expect the killer waves. And there's no way to know the realities of those who were living there, what their thoughts, feelings, or behavior were prior to the calamity.

The point is not to denigrate the immense tragedy, but to draw some lessons not only from the indigenous peoples but also from the animals, who had no doubts about trusting their instincts and no hesitation in responding to these barely perceptible cues and heading for the safety of the higher ground. Perhaps we can draw some lessons from all of this and learn to slow down, breathe, be still, and listen more closely to the various sensations in our bodies, both pleasant and unpleasant. Perhaps we can learn to respect and respond to those physical cues in spite of attempts by our rational mind to disregard these often subtle signals. It's not always an easy thing to do, such as when you have a gut feeling that tells you to be cautious with a new acquaintance, in spite of the fact that everyone in your circle of friends approves of him.

So how do you increase your sensitivity to your instinct? Following are four steps to take to do so:

Breathe—Every so often during your day, take a few moments to pause and consciously take three to four slower, deeper breaths. You'll be surprised at how this can help you be more aware of your physical sensations and also help with the next step, which is . . .

Relax—Not just on a vacation for two weeks out of the year, but daily. Conscious breathing periodically throughout the day will consistently help. It will be a pleasant distraction. When you're uptight and tense, your muscles are contracted in a false state of alertness and your body thinks it's preparing to run or fight. Doing so also helps lower your stress level.

Get Outdoors—Every day, no matter the weather, spend at least a few minutes outside. This helps keep you connect to the natural world.

Observe Animals—Make it a point to get acquainted with the animals near your home, even if it's only the pigeons or squirrels in the nearby park, or the birds that are in the trees close by. Simply observe their habits and behavior through the seasons, and they will teach you.

One of our greatest challenges is not only to find as many ways as possible to pay attention to our instincts, but also to reconnect with the natural world. Doing so helps bring us into greater balance with our rational minds, which has for centuries tended to dominate our world and way of life. Restoring the balance in ourselves will quite naturally lead us to appreciate with greater depth and understanding how we can work in harmony with our Earth Mother and all of her children, to give back to her in gratitude for all that she gives to us.

CHAPTER 19

PISMO THE SNAKE SAVES THE DAY

Pismo was a beautiful Colombian red-tailed boa that I had inherited a few years ago from my daughter, Catherine. She had just moved away from home and didn't have a way to care for her, so this beautiful snake was now mine to care for. I'd already grown quite fond of her by then, and our relationship and mutual respect grew from there.

Snake had already come to me many years prior as an animal spirit guide, so it's no accident that I was given stewardship of a real live snake for a few years. Snake spirit has taught me a tremendous amount about healing, and has been an exceptional spirit guide and counselor.

Pismo once saved my house from catching fire in a most unusual fashion. I was having the carpets cleaned. The cleaner, Mark, had pulled his truck up the incline of the driveway about twenty-five feet from the front door, next to a slope covered with a variety of plants, bushes and a pepper tree. Two floors of the house were directly above where he had parked.

As Mark was cleaning the carpets, I was sequestered in my home office, working on a writing project. I could hear the whine of the carpet-cleaning machine in the truck, a muffled moaning that soon became background noise. After several minutes, I became aware of the absence of this sound and an acrid odor creeping into the room. I left the office and went outside to investigate, and there I saw Mark. He'd returned to his truck, where a trickle of smoke was coming from the rear where the cleaning hose connected to the machine.

When I asked what was happening, Mark explained that as he was cleaning, something urged him to go outside and check on his equipment. When he did, he discovered that the machine had caught fire. As he ran from the front door, he saw a rather large snake slithering away into the bushes on the slope next to the truck. From his description, it sounded like Pismo, but it couldn't have been, as she was still in her cage.

He succeeded in putting out the small fire and shutting down the machine. If he hadn't followed his urge to go outside, it could have been much worse. It may even have caused an explosion, which not only would have damaged a considerable part of our house but could have easily set the house on fire.

I doubt there were any loose boa constrictors roaming around where we live, nor other snakes of that size in our neighborhood. I looked around in the bushes and of course didn't find any. Both of us were shaken by the incident, in particular Mark, yet relieved that any actual danger had been averted.

Had Pismo's spirit appeared to warn Mark? Was she watching out for us and somehow projected her ethereal body that Mark had glimpsed? How did Mark "know" to go out and check the equipment? Although there's no absolute proof for this, after contemplating how this had occurred, I'm convinced that Pismo sent a message to Mark and he picked it up intuitively. I'm certain that Pismo orchestrated this rescue and saved us from what could have been a disastrous situation.

CHAPTER 20

CONVERSATION WITH TURTLE

We've seen a number of calamities throughout the world. Too many to detail all of them, but one that's in our consciousness is Hurricane Irene (August 2011). In a relatively unusual pattern, the storm drifted up the east coast of America and did tremendous damage to many areas in ways that hadn't been seen for many years. Apparently this was in part due to the Atlantic Ocean being a little warmer than usual, thus feeding the hurricane's intensity. In addition we've had a summer of record heat waves, earthquakes, floods, and wildfires here in the United States as well as other parts of the world.

By now there's little or no doubt that we're witness to dramatic changes in the Earth, and can expect these to continue for some time as the planet persists in its balancing act just like it's been doing since its birth over four and a half billion years ago. In that time, the climate has changed countless numbers of times, yet here we are in the midst of one. It just happens that a few billion of us are living on the skin of Gaia and by default we're all involved.

Simultaneously there's an evolutionary progression in our human consciousness as well. Many of us are being called to maintain a conscious alignment with God/Spirit/Creator as much as we possibly can, to not fear the darkness but to *be* the light in the darkness. Even if the darkness inside you in the form of some insidious shadow is attempting to inhibit or completely block your soul's purpose and mission, you can still maintain that critical alignment with your Higher Self.

Before writing this piece I decided to ask Spirit what I should write, so I did a shamanic journey and was taken to Turtle spirit. Turtle has been showing up in a number of ways recently and has become a significant spirit guide the past three weeks, in physical and symbolic form. He started showing up while on our vacation. I was showing Bill and Stephanie the new *Children's Spirit Animal Cards* and pulled one to demonstrate, asking what I needed to know for the trip. It was Turtle saying, "Take your time!" It was a perfect message that continues to resonate.

In the journey, one of the first things he said was:

Slow down! Keep your focus on appreciation and gratitude as much as possible. Yes, the Earth is changing, but it always has been and always will be. As for human beings, since conscious awareness was introduced in your species by the Light Beings thousands of years ago, you now have forgotten that you are merely guests upon this planet. As the eons went on, momentum for this forgetfulness multiplied. You forgot how your ancient ancestors knew so much more than you do now about being in harmony with the Earth.

Turtle went on to offer some other gems of wisdom:

Sometimes your thoughts will manufacture survival situations and react accordingly, when there really isn't one. Most of the time instinct will take care of you. It's part of the design that's meant to help you survive, and coupled with a higher order of logic and reasoning, you can't go wrong. Especially when there's collaboration between instinct and that remarkable gift of human consciousness and reasoning.

When your instinctual responses are triggered by habitual thought patterns based in fear, even though the circumstances don't require such a response, just slow down, breathe, and pay close attention to what's happening in that moment. Look around and notice where you are in the moment. Feel your feet on the ground. Look up at the sky!

A powerful message from Turtle spirit, one that holds promise and hope. I'm reminded also how remarkably adaptive and resourceful we can be as new systems emerge to supplant those that are dissipating. There's so much evidence of not only the evolution of human consciousness but of adaptations that are already taking place, such as the use of natural and sustainable energy resources, the increase in consumption of organic and local foods, and alternative health care for both prevention and healing.

Turtle's counsel to not give in to fear is very wise. As an Earth Sensitive, know that you will feel both the vibrations of the Earth herself as well as the waves of fear and sadness that are pulsating through the collective consciousness, especially whenever there are catastrophic events. That's when it's even more critical to dispel the fear as soon as possible, and return your attention and awareness to the present moment and ideally, to a focus on appreciation and gratitude. Here are ten steps that can work for you.

1) First, check in and see if you are resonating with the fear that is moving through the collective consciousness. As a Sensitive, know that you're more vulnerable to these collective waves of emotion and reactivity.

2) Get out doors, take your shoes and socks off, sit near a tree, and meditate.

3) BREATHE! Learn to use your reactive fear as a trigger for taking three to six slow, deep breaths. It will oxygenate the body, clear your mind, and help you discern what is needed in any particular situation.

4) Talk to someone who will listen and understand what you're saying. Share your feelings without judging them, but don't indulge them more than necessary.

5) Do a walking meditation, if possible barefoot, but if not, leather soled shoes rather than rubber. Walk for five to fifteen minutes at about seventy-five percent of your usual speed. Breathe slowly and steadily.

6) Turn it over to God. One of the principles of any twelve-step recovery program is to do this whenever the urge to drink, smoke, act out, etc. This works for fear too.

7) Gratitude. Make it a point to say "thank you" or other expressions of gratitude and appreciation at least a dozen times each day.

8) Pray. Prayers of thankfulness rather than requests. Bless your food at every meal, taking a few moments and asking that the food before you harmonize with your body and mind.

9) Sing, dance, or indulge in any artistic endeavor. Draw, paint, sculpt or write. Whatever you feel drawn to or feel passionate about.

10) Find space and time to sit in silence for a few minutes to an hour, away from the usual noise that you are so accustomed to hearing.

Choose two or three of these and incorporate them into your spiritual practices. I'd also encourage you to seek signs through divination, paying close attention to signs and omens that are presented to you. Spirit animals are one way to receive information and guidance, as well as ancestors, angels, plant spirits, or any other etheric or physical form that Spirit emanates through.

This era of the shift in human consciousness requires us to align ourselves with Spirit and not get caught up in any rigid doctrine or fundamentalism, but instead learn to attune our internal antenna to the multitude of ways that Spirit seeks to guide and protect us.

Blessings to you all! May God be the guiding force in your life at all times!

CHAPTER 21

ANIMALS, SPIRIT ANIMALS, AND OMENS

I was getting ready to go meet a friend for coffee, feeling a bit wary about the get-together as I had to discuss something unpleasant with him. There was a rumor that he'd made some disparaging remarks about a good friend of mine and I wanted to get the straight scoop from him rather than relying on gossip. I needed to look him in the eye and have a conversation about these allegations, to hear his side of the story. I don't generally like these kinds of confrontations, so even though I was nervous about it, I knew it was important to clear things up directly with him.

As I was getting ready, I glanced out the bedroom window that overlooks a majestic canyon, and saw a hawk cruising along on the air currents. I'd long since learned to pay attention to these appearances by animals as possible messages, but also knew that it wasn't unusual for a hawk to be floating along in this way. I simply noted it and continued getting dressed for the meeting. When I came out of the bathroom, there on the telephone wire about twenty feet from the bedroom window sat that same beautiful red-tailed hawk who only moments before had been gracefully gliding along with the breeze.

"Hmm!" I thought, "I think there's something to this." When an animal appears in an unusual way or repetitively in a short period of time, I take it as an omen or sign. When this happens, it's important to take time to pause and meditate on these appearances, to discern what the message is and its relevance and meaning for the question or concern that is at hand.

The message is actually coming from the spiritual counterpart through the physical presence of the animal. When an animal appears repetitively or in an unusual way, he/she becomes a courier or messenger, passing along the guidance that the spirit of that animal is trying to communicate. So Hawk (the spirit of every single hawk on earth) was attempting to communicate through the red-tailed hawk that had been circling the canyon and was now sitting just a few feet from my eyes. I stopped in my tracks, closed my eyes, took a breath, and silently asked, "Brother Hawk, what are you wanting to tell me?"

Now, once you've asked the question, the response will come in one of four ways: the animal spirit will show you a vision, whisper something to you (typically in very short statements), stimulate a feeling in your body (intuition), or trigger your thinking (insight or inspiration). Often the message comes as a combination of these four channels of spiritual perception.

So, with my eyes closed, I first recalled the image of Hawk circling in the canyon, then my viewpoint switched to seeing from his eyes. Next, a word flashed in my brain— perspective—followed by the thought, "Keep your perspective." That sounded like good advice! It meant stay detached and don't get emotionally wound up about this meeting, before, during, or after.

Staying alert to any further details of this communication, I opened my eyes and simply observed the hawk on the wire. As I did, I was reminded of how patient these winged creatures are. They will stay in one spot for a long time, serene as can be, coolly surveying their surroundings, not worrying or hurrying, taking off only when they're completely ready to do so. The corresponding message, which came as spoken words in my head, was, "Be patient. Let it unfold at a natural pace. Don't jump in right away." This was wise counsel from my spirit animal brother!

As I continued to meditate on Hawk, it occurred to me that not only do hawks have a breadth of vision, but also they're able to focus very quickly and keenly should something attract their attention. Even as they converge their sight on their prospective target, they simultaneously retain the broader perspective. This insight offered another suggestion about how to approach this upcoming conversation with my friend. I interpreted this to mean to keep my perspective, but also listen closely and attentively. I silently thanked Hawk, and the hawk on the wire turned toward me briefly as I did so, as if to say, "You're welcome."

Although I will spare the details of the conversation with my feathered friend, I'm pleased to say the outcome was very positive. I was able to clear some of the gossip that I'd heard, finding out what was true and what wasn't. I remained patient, relaxed and focused throughout, thanks to Hawk's generous and timely advice. A couple of days later I saw that same hawk, once again playing with the currents of the wind, dancing along in the air. I waved to him, and it appeared as if he tipped his wing in response. I took it as a gesture of brotherhood.

This is only one instance of this type of experience. I'm sure you've had a few yourself that have been meaningful and in some instances, life-saving. To receive guidance from the animals it only requires us to be open and receptive. They want to help us, and by our openness, we're helping to restore our right relationship with the natural world.

Truly, the animals are our brothers and sisters. We must respect them as such, view them that way, and be willing to allow them to teach us, guide us, and heal us. One of the most powerful ways they do this is when they serve as animal spirit guides, whether for a few moments, or for a lifetime.

The following four pieces are communications from Raven that I received in shamanic journeys, asking what he wanted to say to all people. These are unedited and raw, as I transcribed them.

CHAPTER 22

RAVEN SPEAKS

*The following are unedited downloads of messages I
received from Raven spirit on four different occasions.*

December 5, 2008

Let's face it. We're in an era of deconstruction. Concepts
tumbling down like bricks falling from an indentured wall.
World events that when viewed collectively, overwhelm
the senses. Constant bombardment of news, the raiments
of civilization advertising as pleasing or pretty or better
than the previous one, buy now! Take ten percent off.

Nature has a way of thinning out the predators of her
precious body, the virus that has been consuming her
body and her being. That virus is the human being, all
"evolved" and arrogant beyond belief.

Take the darkness and from it birth the light. That's quite a
trick but it's happening all the time. As a human being,
you've become as a species so complacent with these
amazing powers rooted in an evolution of consciousness
that is still housed in a monkey body. And much more
reactive to the instinctual and species-specific traits than
you would dare admit.

This plus being perpetually dissociated from your true relationship with the natural world. More is better requires because there's more of you than ever before. The skin of our Earth Mother has been mottled, dug into, burned, bombed, and totally wired into the complexity of your so-called civilization.

You view nature from inside your glass sliding door. You still have shards of the fear based on the limitations of your physical body, needing to shield yourself from the wild and uncertain vagaries of nature.

February 24, 2009

Caw! Caw! Sing! Sing! This is the time to sing! Doesn't matter whether you do so in the shower, church choir, rock and roll band, by yourself, or with others. Sing without concern for structure or form, or in particular, how it's going to sound. Challenge yourself! Lose your inhibitions!

Okay, can't do it because of the economy? Look at how the meaning of that word has changed so much in just a few short months. Are you reading all the horror stories? Are you plugged into the radio and/or the television for more than an hour? What news programs do you listen to or watch? Where do you get your news?

Wherever it is, turn off the radio, the television, and don't read the news *anywhere*, including the internet. I dare you. Try it for a week and see what happens. A news abstinence.

What is happening is that a constant stream of information is coming your way through computers, cell phones, and most notoriously, much of the time your brain. Your brain—specifically your "Automatic Mind"—is notorious for directing your attention elsewhere other than here at this moment, as the thoughts drone on in the background, just at the edge of your awareness.

You've heard the expression, "garbage in, garbage out," sometimes acronymically—if that's even a word—GIGO. And this is never more accurate when we speak of the information that you allow in through our senses. You're constantly processing information that comes through your eyes, ears, physical sensations, and especially your instinct, which is how your body runs the very basic equipment and provides the know-how necessary for survival.

Your instinct is so powerful yet so ignored. Learn to pay attention to your instinct. Just get quiet and listen closely to your body. You're going to have to slow down and breathe to do that.

March 31, 2009

Trials and tribulations. 2012 fears. Look at those little birds outside your back door, dancing with spring like there was no tomorrow. And in fact for them there is no tomorrow. Only now. Living in it is more than a discipline or a philosophy. Living in the now means you completely let go of your usual mind, this Automatic Mind that you've been referring to and shift fully into the Awakening Mind. The Awakening Mind is something to call the Self that is fully focused in the present moment. Awareness shifts. Fact of life.

But you humans have this remarkable capacity to think ahead and imagine what's there, or how things should go, or what to have for dinner tomorrow. Me, I just go get dinner. Instinct rules. Not in a way that doesn't have some meaning for acting in a proper way. Every animal on Earth acts in a proper way. There is no impropriety. There is no sin amongst the animals. There are codes of behavior, structured in a way that accords with the species instinct and culture, yet with room for the ebb and flow of other influences, particular information of the senses that dictate how the instinct will operate in any given situation.

As they say, there is no future in that. No anticipation and ultimately, no anxiety. That's a human invention and term when the nervous system gets anxiety out of proportion to the events that are occurring in that person's life. Oh, yeah, animals get activated already. Typically and purely as a means of pursuing safety, pleasure, or nourishment. The rabbit will be wide-eyed and run at almost anything that appears to be threatening. Why? Because rabbits are a very popular prey. That's why there's so many of them and they reproduce at an amazingly fast rate.

Same with the concept of "past." Really, what's done is done. There ain't no going back. There is no "back" there! It's all memory kicking in, sometimes very detailed and sometimes largely obscure and subconscious.

See, I know what you're all about. Because I am both human and I am Raven. Which one is talking now?

May 20, 2010

As I fly upon this Earth, making my way across the land I see nothing but beauty. It troubles us that you human beings are so focused on your fears. So many people are worried about his and that. The Creator of All that moves through us and as us with breath delights in both the dark and the light. Look at my blackness. Does that make you nervous? Does it challenge you, just like the shadows of humankind that show themselves to you in others and in yourself?

Welcome those shadows, for it is the light of awareness when shed upon them that, no, doesn't dissolve them, but just reveals what needs to be revealed. The shadows of addictions, greed, secrecy, righteousness, hate, envy— own them! Don't let them rule you, but own them. One of the gifts I as Raven spirit bring is helping you bring those shadows into the Light to be integrated so you can more completely accept your humanity and your divinity.

You humans separate the light and the dark, thinking that it's somehow bad to be "in the dark." Yet do not fear the darknesses in you or others. Embrace them and watch what happens. By accepting these very human characteristics, you find understanding and compassion. There but for the grace of the Creator go I. Often said, but not often felt deeply. Not out of arrogance or a holier-than-thou frame, but from a place of deep compassion for not only your fellow human travelers, but all travelers on this planet.

Grace. Finding peace in grace. What does that really mean? Means to be aligned with Spirit, to be at one with all these aspects, to truly feel in your heart of hearts, even if only moments at a time, the truth of who you are: intimately intertwined and connected to All-That-Is. You are the Creator. The Creator is you. You are Creation. Creation is you. You are all of the Creator and Creation embodied as YOU.

Duality exists only in your mind. Unity exists in your heart.

REFERENCES

Farmer, Steven, *Animal Spirit Guides*, Hay House Inc, US, 2006.

Farmer, Steven, Earth Magic, "The Grasshopper Sings 'Let the Song Find You'," <http://www.earthmagic.net/shamanic-journey/the-grasshopper-sings-let-the-song-find-you/> viewed March 13, 2017.

Farmer, Steven, *Healing Ancestral Karma*, Hierophant Publishing, San Antonio, 2014.

ALSO BY
Dr. Steven Farmer

THE SHAMAN'S PATH message cards

70 Affirmation Cards with instructions for use

www.AnimalDreamingPublishing.com

ABOUT THE AUTHOR

Dr. Steven Farmer is world-renowned author, teacher, licensed psychotherapist, and Shamanic Healer. His books and other products include *Healing Ancestral Karma, Earth Magic®, Earth Magic® Oracle Cards, Animal Spirit Guides, Pocket Guide to Spirit Animals, Sacred Ceremony, Power Animal Oracle Cards, Messages from Your Animal Spirit Guides Oracle Cards, Power Animals, Messages from Your Animal Spirit Guides guided meditation CD,* and the soon to be released *Shaman's Path* Cards. For children, he has produced the *Children's Spirit Animal Cards* (with Jesseca Camacho-Farmer) and *Children's Spirit Animal Stories CD vols I and II.*

In addition to workshops on Healing Ancestral Karma, Animal Spirit Guides, Shamanism, Shamanic Breathwork, and earth-centered spirituality, Dr. Farmer offers private consultations for Psychospiritual and Shamanic Healing and Soul Readings in person or remotely by phone, Skype, or Zoom. He also offers the nine month Earth Magic® Practitioner Certification training, the Spiritual Mentorship program, and Personal Intensives for individual and couples.

For more information about private sessions, special events and workshops please visit his website: http://EarthMagic.net or Facebook page: http://www.facebook.com/pages/Dr-Steven-Farmer/9301885258